THE LEARNING CENTRE

D0487433

Stock no. 02249

Class
914
.206
CON

Labels

SOLIHULL SIXTH FORM COLLEGE
THE LEARNING CENTRE

Beside the Seaside

JOSEPH CONNOLLY

with colour photography by Joe Cornish

Rec RECEIVED 2 0 MAR 2002

Stock no. 02249

Class

394.
26
(CON)

T ✓ G.   L+T

CHECKED   JUL 2008

CHECKED   NOV 2002

Mitchell Beazley

BESIDE THE SEASIDE
by Joseph Connolly
with colour photography by Joe Cornish

First published in Great Britain in 1999
by Mitchell Beazley, an imprint of
Octopus Publishing Group Ltd,
2-4 Heron Quays, London E14 4JB

Copyright © Octopus Publishing Group Ltd 1999
Text copyright © Joseph Connolly 1999

All rights reserved. No part of this work may
be reproduced or utilised in any form or by
any means, electronic or mechanical, including
photocopying, recording or by any information
storage and retrieval system, without the prior
written permission of the publisher.

The author has asserted his moral rights.

ISBN 184 000 164X

A CIP catalogue record for this book is available
from the British Library.

The author and publisher will be grateful for
any information that will assist them in keeping
future editions up to date. Although all reasonable
care has been taken in the preparation of this
book, neither the publishers nor the author
can accept liability for any consequences arising
from the use thereof, or from the information
contained therein.

Commissioning Editor: Margaret Little
Editor: Hilary Lumsden
Design: Lovelock & Co.
Picture Research: Claire Gouldstone
Production: Paul Hammond
Index: Ann Barrett

Typeset in Gill Sans, Garamond, Helvetica.

Printed and bound by
Toppan Printing Company in China.

Contents

This happy bevy of bathers at Eastbourne in 1930 would like to extend the warmest of welcomes – to invite you to join them, beside the seaside. Wish you were here? You already are. Come on in – the water's lovely…

Introduction

The seaside – don't you just love it? Most people seem to cherish the odd fond memory of a long ago holiday at some sunny resort or other. Even the trips that turned out to be disasters are often recounted amid gales of a self-deprecating laughter. This, of course, is a very British trait – the firm belief that when you are beside the seaside, although actual pain or violent death are best on the whole avoided, the occasional inconvenience or discomfort is positively beneficial to the soul. Why else would entire families struggle to erect not just deeply uncooperative deck-chairs, but a furiously flapping wind-break in the midst of the sort of wind that quite clearly will never be broken? Or doggedly consume bridge rolls in which the crunch of cucumber is easily outdone by that of the layer of sand?

Back in the 1950s and 1960s, even staying in the variety of boarding house that would make a concentration camp seem warmly welcoming and snugly cosy was stoically taken on board as all part and parcel of the Great British seaside experience.

All these little niggles, however, paled to insignificance when put alongside the countless good bits that a seaside holiday has to offer; with anticipation during the journey down accounting for a fair deal of the heady euphoria that the killer combination of sun, sea and sand can so effortlessly infect you with. Seaside fun is highly contagious. John Betjeman captured some of this in a poem of 1941, with the very same title as the book you are now holding: *Beside the Seaside*.

The real-life bathing beauties opposite are soaking up the rays at Bexhill, Sussex, and – in true British fashion – are not remotely fazed by the discomfort of shingle. The only shingle below, though, is on the heads of this pair of idealised lovelies, in an early 1920s example of the classic seaside postcard as reinvented by Donald McGill.

The caption – less saucy than usual – runs as follows: "They say terrible things about him and the worst of it is they're all true, I'm happy to say." McGill – a priceless one-man seaside institution – once admitted in an interview: "I'm really a serious-minded man underneath".

Thank goodness that underneath is where his serious-mindedness remained.

Ah, young love. What could be more romantic at the end of another warm, sunlit and perfect day on the beach than tearing off your sandals in a fit of abandon, rolling up those flannels, and strolling into the dusk with the girl of your dreams? One feels sure that for these two, the summer of 1952 would ever remain the sweetest of memories.

Father's toes
Though now encased in coloured socks and shoes
And pressing the accelerator hard,
Ache for the feel of sand and little shrimps
To tickle in between them. Mother vows
To be more patient with the family;
Just for its sake she will be young again.
And, at that moment, Jennifer is sick…

Well there you are. Nobody actually promised us that the family seaside holiday would be utterly perfect (and past experience, you would feel safe in assuming, might surely give us an inkling). But, everyone is more than willing to buy into the *idea* of the thing. In the days when trains were the only practical way of actually getting to the seaside (and any aspirant resort that lacked a station simply curled up and died a death) people gazed at the stunning array of railway holiday posters and – elbowing aside all reason – believed in what they saw. Kingfisher-blue sky (check), golden sand (check) and a Cary Grant and Grace Kelly of a couple, with a sweet and matching pair of dreamy children (the sturdy boy quite properly taller than the girl, who was always a strawberry blonde). And – get this – *no one else on the beach at all.* (Not only that: the sandcastles looked like they had been fashioned over a period of years by Sir Christopher Wren.)

The reality, of course, was just a wee bit different – but no less fun for that. And if it does cloud over and come on to rain, we can always go on the pier and lose loads of money on silly machines. While we're there we can buy some rock and nibble on that, then have an ice-cream cornet, possibly a few cockles and maybe a toffee apple, and round it all off with a nice cup of tea ("ooh – I think that tea was a mistake, you know – I feel a bit … Oh look: the sun's out again. Let's all go and sit on a donkey!")

This band of pretty little budding bathing beauties from 1909 are just happy to do what comes naturally, when beside the seaside. All they need – apart from this dazzling array of headgear – are the sun, the sea and the sand (not forgetting that rather classy bucket).

The incomparable and rather alluring seafront at Blackpool, just as the sun fades away and the town's fantastic illuminations begin to take over. In high season, Blackpool rarely sleeps: the tower, the pier and the prom will all be busy for hours and hours to come, the typical visitor to this resort being wholly determined to party till late.

And although we talk generically of "the seaside", in truth every resort is different from the next – each of them has a very singular character of its own. The holiday-maker whose idea of a cracking good time is a gorgeously gaudy fortnight in Blackpool is not going to be best pleased by the elegant restraint of Hove, nor by publess Frinton. Similarly, for the fanatical surfers at Newquay, Southend – for all its charms – just isn't going to cut it; and the nudist beach at Brighton is maybe not quite the thing if Southwold is what you're used to.

The whole big point of the seaside is freedom – an inalienable right to do exactly what you please, whenever you damn well like. Whether it be the wearing of huge and unfeasibly floral dresses or the itsy-bitsy-teeny-weeniest yellow polka-dot bikini, and to battle with changing out of them behind a couple of towels, held up by someone annoying who sniggers a lot and keeps on threatening to whisk them away. You can buy rude, jokey or traditional mega-Technicolor postcards, and not actually send them until the very last day because it's such a terrible bore queuing up for the stamps. You can also buy a lime-green plastic bucket and fill this with wet sand for no very obvious reason at all. And if you want a fortune teller to tell you only that fortune is coming your way, well then the seaside is very much the place to do it.

Another area offering a great deal of scope for idiosyncrasy is that of the seaside souvenir. The only rules to follow here are that anything you buy must be totally useless, poorly constructed, wildly overpriced and in the worst possible taste. (As I say, there is a great deal of scope). This applies too even if you are buying for yourself. Do so with confidence, and in the certainty that you won't actually have to live with your crested china piggy, perched on the rim of a lavatory and perusing a late edition of Pork Times, because it will be chucked to the back of a cupboard along with all the junk you hauled home last year.

The rather wonderful array of photographs that follows (treats to come; oh, indeed, what larks!) allows you to wallow in a comforting nostalgia all of your own. Just about every single aspect of the seaside holiday is vividly recalled, the time span extending from the final days of the nineteenth century practically up to the end of our own. Whichever decade best sums up for you the bliss and brass of the seaside holiday surely has to be in here somewhere. So all that remains now is for you to set aside everything else and come and join me, beside the seaside.

Possibly the best-known and best-loved pier in Britain – Palace Pier, at Brighton. There's just something about this Sussex resort that perfectly sums up the quintessential seaside experience: the town's effortless blend of posh and vulgar, sedate and racy; the wildly expensive jostling for space amid the cheap and cheerful. Brighton's got the lot.

Piers and Promenades

In every resort in Britain, the sea itself is the star of the show, but it just wouldn't be the same without the grand and lavish promenades, studded with bandstands and shelters, all fringed by pastel-coloured and decorative ironwork – and even more especially the wondrous projections of the piers. These together epitomise the fun and frivolity of the seaside holiday. It never palls: the thrill of being able to amble hundreds of yards out to sea and then – having lost a fistful of change on a silly machine – turning to view the resort itself, all that way away.

And here, above, is a splendid clutch of sunshine girls, doing just that very thing. It is the summer of 1949, they are clustered close to the end of Eastbourne Pier and making the most of the sublime and awesomely distant view of the front and the packed-out beaches. (See overleaf for a modern view of the pier itself.) The 1950s picture to the right – by legendary *Picture Post* photographer Bert Hardy –

is justly famous, summing up, as it does, the bracing combination of sun and sea breezes. The image is quite gently spiced by just a hint of naughty seaside abandon. You may be sure that the blonde and more animated of the pair of girls is rather gratified by the upshot of sudden coastal gusts: this girl needed to be noticed, which is maybe why she borrowed the polka-dot number from Minnie Mouse in the first place.

To the left we have a rare 1920s view of the promenade at Sidmouth, Devon. Briefly fashionable as early as the 1820s as a result of a flurry of royal patronage, Sidmouth's star somewhat waned in the latter part of the nineteenth century. This was due to the fact that railways had yet to stretch this far, and a station in those days was seen to be absolutely vital to the lifeblood and future of any resort.

All that was soon to change, and Sidmouth – with, as may be seen from the picture, its very singular front and setting – became again a rather select and popular resort, the balmy climate being much recommended by Harley Street to the infirm or anyone with respiratory problems. Contemporary reports suggest that during high season the front was practically lined with crow-like black bath chairs and invalid carriages, many of their occupants, with huge deliberation, dutifully sucking down great lungfuls of Nature's own cure, and then hacking with violence to the point of a seizure.

We assume, however, that the girls above on Brighton's Palace Pier in 1946, are not the victims of a terminal coughing fit. Not dead at all, in fact, but simply, during that first summer of peace for more than six years, succumbing to the effects of the wonderful combination of sunshine and leisure, boosted maybe by the after-effects of a slap-up lunch with all the trimmings, and possibly just the one cherry brandy to follow. Could they all be dreaming of the tall, dark, handsome stranger that Gypsy Petulengro promised solemnly, to each of them, they would one day surely meet?

The town of Saltburn in North Yorkshire is these days what might be termed a well-kept secret, but when they started building it from scratch in 1861, the idea was that as a seaside resort it should equal nearby Scarborough. As may be seen from the two spreads following overleaf – the first a sweeping panorama of Scarborough bay in 1911, the second a modern and rather unusual view of the town's breakwater and Coastguard Station – it fell somewhat short of its ambition. Nevertheless, the moving of the railway from neighbouring Redcar and the construction of a series of gentle scenic pathways down to the beach (not to say a short-lived and death-defying steel cage that plummeted vertically from a height of 250 feet) Saltburn made quite a name for itself in its heyday as a somewhat genteel resort, catering to what was locally termed the "upper crust".

The pier – to the right and below – came in 1869, and although the 620 foot-long structure is the original Victorian cast ironwork, the pier was once three times as long as this, and culminated in a bandstand. A series of storms and errant ships down the decades put paid to all that, though, and now there is just a bare and exposed platform at the sea head, much loved by local anglers. (There is mackerel by the bucketload to be had, apparently.)

The mock Tudor buildings on the shore-end are as recent as 1910, and now house a battery of clanking video games (sometimes it's open, sometimes it's not). This is frequented by the oldies as well as thrill-crazy youngsters – maybe partially for the reason that in Saltburn we have a Quaker town, and even now there is only one proper pub. It opened in the 1970s, and is popular.

CAUTION
Barriers may close
without warning

When closed,approach
slowly for automatic
opening,this side only

Southend, above, really took off – in common with so many other southern resorts – around the 1880s. This was a direct result of not only the expansion of the railways, but also the fact that 80 per cent of London workers now received a phenomenal and long-dreamt-of windfall: a paid summer holiday. The pier, pictured here in 1948, was one of the very first in Britain to install a miniature tramcar to clankingly convey the happy ranks of paying customers the very length of it, and – after a suitable interval devoted to shooting wonky and half-fledged arrows at impenetrable butts, or maybe aiming elliptical rifle barrels at a fast-moving flotilla of pock-marked tinplate ducks – all the way back again.

Further along the coast (and to the left), that very same summer of 1948, we have a solitary seagull surveying the scene over Hastings Pier. This dramatically foreshortened view packs in a good deal of the treats on offer: the main attraction this year being daily concerts featuring none other than Hector Davies (and his band).

Just how different the settings for Britain's piers can be. On the right is a rocky strand hard by Llandudno Pier, in North Wales. Above is a very famous kiosk in Brighton on Palace Pier, for a long time the entrance booth to the pier itself. But these days it has become possibly the tiniest art gallery in the world, apparently specialising in rather cutesy portrayals of folk got up in Edwardian bathing costumes. Less than a mile down the coast is the stretch of sand where people wear absolutely nothing at all (nostalgia meets daring innovation, a common collision at the seaside). Sometimes there is a silhouette cutter on the pier, a form of seaside souvenir dating back to the Regency. Among the current bestselling mementos are giant, fluorescent inflatable hammers (don't ask), shakeable glass summer beach snow globes (don't think) and small ceramic ashtrays bearing the Brighton crest, each lovingly crafted in the form of a lavatory (don't speak).

And here – as if it were needed – is proof positive that just occasionally during the course of the summer seaside holiday, the sun declines to put in an appearance. Certainly, in these shots, it seems to be sulking with a vengeance – but the gent, seen above, in 1953 is putting a typically brave and British face on it. Forget the rain – just adjust the trilby to a rakish angle and attempt to strike up a conversation with the similarly wind-whipped and head-scarfed young lady, while drawing deep on a comforting ciggie (you're never alone on the strand). On Worthing Pier to the right, in 1949, it is a similar scene of desolation and, generally speaking, not much is happening at all. Maybe they're collecting up the deckchairs in order to stoke up a jolly good bonfire (but not, we hope, on the wood-decked pier).

Brighton may safely be credited with the invention of the pier as not so much a landing jetty, but more a way of holiday life. The magnificent and innovative Chain Pier was built in 1822. It was so called because it resembled a sort of truncated suspension bridge (leading, of course, to nowhere), made up of four stone towers and hung with steel support cables. The entertainment side of the Chain Pier grew as souvenir and tea shops gradually opened along its length, and fireworks became a sizzling feature. Thackeray was one of the few, though, who didn't grumble about the entrance fee: "Here for the sum of twopence," he wrote, "you can go out to sea and pace this vast deck without need of a basin".

In 1866, however, West Pier (left and above) rose up from the sea, bang opposite the very select Regency Square, much to the undisguised horror of its very superior inhabitants. Fashion-conscious trippers, being what they are, deserted the Chain Pier wholesale in favour of this new and brassier delight. By the 1890s, the old Chain Pier was scheduled for demolition, but was swept away to sea instead during the great storm of 1896. On its site was built the present Palace Pier, probably now the most famous and best-loved in Britain.

West Pier – though still popular – was always Number Two from then onwards, though the semi-derelict structure you see here is a result of yet another of these fearsome storms, this one as recent as 1975. It was closed and declared unsafe, whereupon Brighton immediately rekindled its affection for the old thing. For more than 20 years various schemes have been mooted and discarded to restore the West Pier to its former glory. At the time of writing, it looks like this might finally happen, although 2002 is the earliest projected date for the eventual grand reopening.

The easy glamour of the seaside, dressed for an evening on the town. Compare the above 1935 shot of Scarborough with the sunlit present-day view on page 81. Rather gratifyingly – and this is why we keep on coming back to the seaside – in the intervening 60 or so years, virtually nothing has changed at all. And, fashions apart, much the same may be said of Palace Pier, Brighton (right), in 1959. (No matter how glorious your day on the beach has been, it still gets rather chilly in the evening, you know – so don't forget to wrap up warm.)

The seaside is different at night. Exciting, yes, but there can be just a hint of unseen danger too (especially if you are lurking beneath Palace Pier as the black water slurps at the shore, and you have just finished reading *Brighton Rock* by Graham Greene. You certainly don't require to meet anyone even half-way approaching Pinkie at this time of night, thank you.) It is maybe because you can hear the swell and rush of the sea, but you can't quite make it out. The lights that shimmer into it serve only to distort, and you cannot come to terms with its vastness. None of which, of course, matters a jot when you've laughed yourself silly at some quite cheeky show in the pier theatre. Next on the agenda is a cracking fish supper, and maybe also a nip of something strong – should the cockles of your heart need further warming. (Overleaf is an atmospheric shot of a very different pier indeed – that at Whitby, in North Yorkshire.)

Bathing Beauties

The striking and wonderful feature about bathing beauties is that they don't ever bathe. They wear the costume – oh but of course (and where else but the seaside can you get away with so little and not be arrested?). But this is almost always accessorised: high-heeled shoes are good, while wide-brimmed hats and parasols are not to be sneezed at. Failing that, maybe just a thoughtful cigarette, or, the perennial favourite, pointedly gazing just anywhere except towards the gangs of people ogling you. It is called cool – and the beach just wouldn't be the same without it.

We have here two very different approaches to being the absolute focus of attention. The three lovelies in Llandudno, above, in this rather evidently carefully posed and oh-so-titillating 1935 shot ("now left leg forward, ladies!") may or may not be intent on the naughty flicker-vision they each have invested a penny to see. (The girl nearest to us has plumped for an epic called "Hubby Sweetie".) But they know full well that they themselves are very much the stars of the show. The rather more earthy young thing to the right, however, is using the shingle on Brighton beach to huge advantage: is there a couple of strapping young lads who will help me to the sea and spare my little tootsies? Why yes – there always is, isn't there? As every bathing beauty knows. An interesting sidelight here is that all three of them appear to be wearing precisely the same costume: that's 1927 for you.

Don't be fooled: at first glance, it very much appears as if the girl above, at Brighton in 1929, is poised on breaking the golden rule for all bathing *belles* by actually getting wet, thereby rendering the jersey swimsuit not just unshapely but about ten pounds heavier (the potential damage by sea water to the latest bob, crop or shingle being too much even to contemplate). No, she's not really going to dive, because look – she's still got her shoes on. The pose is solely for the benefit of the photographer and posterity, and we can now be properly grateful to both. Shoes, of course, are very necessary on Brighton beach, as anyone who has ever crashed and stumbled over the hot stones will tell you.

The two exceedingly emancipated young would-be flappers alongside are actually in Lowestoft, also in the 1920s, but they have clearly embraced the principle. (The bandanna on the girl to the right is, I assure you, merely wet-look as opposed to actually wet.) And those cigarettes! Just too cool for words – but how long have they been striving for a light? One hopes that they were well stocked up with Bryant & May, because this close to the sea, I'm afraid, just the one box simply won't do the trick.

The nuns to the left must surely have stood out, that day in Frinton back in the 1950s. However, 75 years earlier, they would have merited not so much as a second glance, because wimples apart, this is much how a respectable middle-class woman would have appeared for a day out on the beach. Certainly the sisters were in the right resort: Frinton prizes decorousness above all things, bar maybe sobriety.

The nuns are clearly determined that no sun's ray whatsoever will get anywhere close to them. This could hardly be said for the ladies above: they are seated somewhat masochistically on what has to be the nastiest section of Torquay's generally gorgeous beach. And no, they are not remotely contemplating casting aside brolly and cavorting in the sea (note the perms and earrings). But here's a thought. All these good women are British, and they are no strangers to the ins and outs of a summer's day beside the seaside. Maybe they heard on the BBC forecast that it could well turn showery later, and here is no more than a classic case of being prepared.

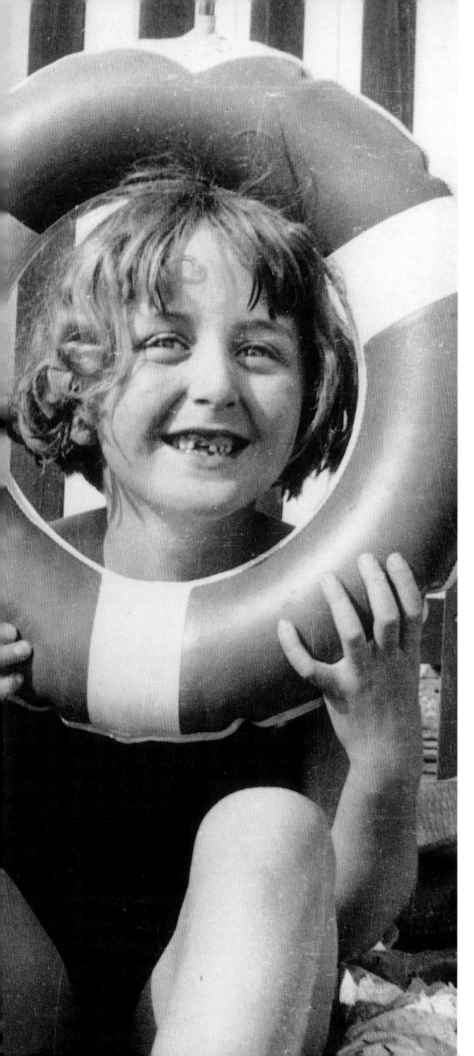

The previous page positively exults in the wonderful carefree abandon shared by a quintet of very happy young things at Brighton in the 1920s. It's the sight of youth having such simple, clean and terribly good fun that really brings the seaside alive. Just look at the unstoppable holiday grins on these pages (Brighton again – ten years later). Very much one for the album.

This just about perfect seaside snap was taken in 1934, the very year when inflatable beach toys – and most particularly blow-up air beds – first made their mark. Instantly popular as not just swimming aids (or at least anti-drowning aids) but friendly missiles to chuck at people's heads. How the children chortled gleefully while forcing out the air from a rubber ring, in roguish anticipation of the jolly rude noises to come.

Inflatables may have reached their acme of popularity in the 1950s, when a quite common seaside sight was a purple-faced father near palsied as a result of his valiant attempts to blow hoarsely into some flaccid and amorphous coloured plastic shape – tasting of salt and gritty with sand – praying that soon it would expand into some form or other, and preferably not at the cost of his very last breath on earth.

I once saw a little girl clambering on to a large pink and green inflatable seahorse in the shallows at Brighton. Each time she did so the horse ducked and threw her, whereupon she laughed quite hysterically and attempted to remount. Again, the horse would effortlessly get the better of her – but this time, alarmingly, it burst. The little girl burst into floods of tears and her mother rushed to console her with a large Mister Whippy cornet, with crammed-in double Cadbury's Flake. She laughed again, ringingly, and toddled off happily to bury her daddy right up to his neck.

A solitary man can be quite happy on the beach – skimming stones, say, or maybe gathering seashells – then along comes a girl such as one of these and he wonders quite frankly why he bothers.

The combination of glamour and sun can be quite a dazzler, as surely each of these beauties knows quite well. The very chic young woman to the left, together with the masted vessel, give this picture a decidedly Continental air, but in fact the scene is early 1950s Southend (not too typical, though). Above, we have Eastbourne – but, the original caption informs us dryly, the girl is French.

Mais evidemment! The tan, the bikini, the Bardot-esque pout – to say nothing of the perfectly painted finger and toenails. Oh yes, this is French all right. And true, the said bikini even betrays traces of authentic sea water – but only commensurate with having sprinted with grace along the shoreline and kicked up a tantalising and crystal spray – far more photogenic than anything so crude as actual immersion. (From the point of view of the buildings behind her, she certainly lends a rather refreshing twist to the populist term "a room with a view".)

But bathing *belles* are not only the lovesome things to be seen on the beach – let's hear it now for the chaps! To our right, at Brighton, we have a fellow who takes the seaside very seriously indeed – stiff collar, boots and bowler: no concessions whatever to sea 'n' surf, let along sunnin' and funnin'.

But this is August 1939, and so to be fair, he has a lot on his mind: as may be inferred from his newspaper, war is just weeks away. And here is a man who well remembers the '14–'18 show. Can Britain pull it off again? Will our beloved seaside become just the first foothold on the road to invasion by the Hun? No no – if it comes to it, we will (just as Winston Churchill said later we would) fight them on the beaches. The gentleman's wife in the background, it must be said, seems to be taking an altogether more pragmatic view of the global situation, as well she might: if it comes, it comes – meanwhile, let's just doze in the shade.

The pictures above and overleaf were taken in Blackpool in 1956. While the fellow above is possibly lost in contemplation over what life can hold for him, now that he has a Yorkshire terrier growing out of his chest, the lads overleaf seem more intent on having a rocking good time, as only 1950s youth knew how. They've got the quiffs, the Roy Rogers hats, and they're damned if they're removing their socks – so let the good times roll.

Life on the Beach

The beach – that magical 6,000 mile ribbon of sand and shingle that encircles Britain and is viewed quite properly as a vital part of our national birthright. All things are possible on the beach: inhibitions and sartorial standards are not so much lowered as eagerly abandoned. Children rush off to do whatever comes naturally, while adults – filled with their own golden memories of all those rosy and youthful seaside jaunts that blur into one – are not too far behind them. On the beach, all you have to do is just go with the summer flow.

There are no age limits on the beach – here is everyone's playground. In the early days, however, things were rather more decorous. These young girls above (c.1910) demonstrate not only glowing and rude good health and the ability to quite literally let their hair down when the occasion demands, but also a fair grasp of the principles of fielding. The adaptation of formal town umbrellas into makeshift stumps says a good deal about the "hey gang – let's do the show right here" way of thinking that often comes over a group on the beach. Games, parties, competitions – they all just seem to happen. Where else could an elderly man – 40 years on – take it into his head to remove his trousers and happily display, to the evident delight of all the onlookers, not just his taste in hosiery, but also his indisputably knobbly knees?

Here we see, in all its glory, not just the splendour of the seaside bandstand, but also – in the very recent picture to the right, taken at Eastbourne – its continued popularity. For many holiday-makers, it is enough to catch the odd fading cadence of tuba or bassoon as it is wafted high by sea breezes; the satisfaction of knowing that the brass band is alive and well and giving it all it's got from under its coolly elegant cupola.

For others – the true fans – the full recital must be witnessed in its entirely, and prime seats are prized (not in the full glare of the sun, though: it can roast you in August, you know). There is much syncopated tapping of feet, wrists and walking sticks, as heads bob up and down in time to the rousing score.

The beautiful and delicate filigree of the above example in Brighton always makes for a fine silhouette at just about any time of the day. I well remember a jolly little concert here when I was a lad. The audience just loved it when the band struck up "Oh I Do Like To Be Beside The Seaside…!" and I, along with everyone else, had a great time chiming in with all the "Tiddley-Om-Pom-Poms!"

Golden days.

This veritable Armada of "floating beds" as they were called (previous pages) was captured at Margate in 1934 – just out that year and a huge and immediate hit – as the contagiously happy faces on all those lucky people amply show. Did any of them ever forget that wonderful summer?

In contrast, it is possible that the lady on the right did her best to blank out all memory of Bournemouth in 1954 – one of the worst summers the resort recorded. But she demonstrates true grit and a proper understanding of the English seaside holiday in adversity: it must be got through. She would not sit in her winter coat in the garden, no – but on the beach, it is perfectly acceptable. And indeed, if you have already paid for the day's hire of a deck-chair, quite essential; it's the same principle as insisting on finishing an ice-cream covered in sand – it's simply a question of getting your money's worth.

The man above at Blackpool the same year seemed to fare better. Certainly he had the right idea: you do things on the beach that are inconceivable anywhere else. Smiling benignly as a child buries you alive, say, or buying a very silly hat and actually wearing it. Men in particular can become utterly engrossed while constructing a multi-parapet and crenellated wonderland out of sand and sea water, as well as carefully fashioning flags out of plastic spoons and slivers of lolly wrapper. Then comes the sheer thrill of the dug-out conduit, thereby flooding the moat. This chap, though, has gone for the more casual approach. While his kiddy romps safely under the mother's watchful eye, he elects to roll up his suit trousers, sit in the pram and dunk his feet in a cooling puddle of mud. The residual sand will lurk in his socks and shoes for months to come.

Ah yes, that other vital part of our collective memory of seaside summers gone by: the holiday romance. Now for this you need an altogether less crowded and maybe more elevated section of beach – as the couple above in Plymouth in 1954 seems to have discovered for themselves – or maybe a secret and magical time of day: dawn or dusk. The annual two weeks off that most people this young could have expected in those days were, of course, endlessly precious. There was, quite simply, no time to lose.

Once more the ozone and the feeling of freedom that the seaside unerringly confers came hugely into play. The repressions of home and the workplace dissolved into the sun, helped along by the fact that people wore a good deal less than they did in the High Street at home.

Here, the young man has discarded both tie and cufflinks (!) while the clearly receptive girl has opted for a rather chic bolero jacket to offset the pretty racy swimsuit. The combination of smiles, laughter and the common imperative to have a good time served to bring many people together. And when the aching time came to part, they took home with them not just the crested ashtray, kewpie doll or plaster Alsatian won at the fun-fair, but the memory too of that so special song, just written for the two of them, and that wondrous time when they ran hand in hand through the sun-dappled surf.

Afterwards came the exchange of cherished addresses and the avowals to write every day, for here could be no mere holiday romance. This was the real thing – this was forever.

The sheer exhilarating expanse of some stretches of coastline can be quite literally breathtaking. All that space and all that sky serve to encourage horseplay and make physical high jinks seem virtually a necessity, particularly when no one else is around and the whole of the beach belongs to you. For the girl above, in St Leonards in 1936, nothing else in the world exists beyond this tug of war with her dog, who is loving every moment.

To the left, we have a rare 1925 view of Brighton at low tide, a couple of months before high season. The town had yet to be engulfed by holiday-makers, all the London workers still wishfully ticking off the days until the time would come for their own special week in the sun. The young people here are (evidently active) members of the Brighton Swimming Club whose aim, in theory, was to take the plunge every single day. But, judging by their dress, the girls seem a good deal more into the spirit of the idea than the lads do (as, at the seaside, can often be the way).

Overleaf are a few holiday-makers indulging in an altogether less strenuous pastime: strolling. The seaside is just made for strolling – and particularly when there are backdrops such as this to gladden the eye: splendidly maintained twin cupolas on the promenade at Bexhill, Sussex. Though not so racy or prominent as some resorts, it was nonetheless Bexhill that led the way in giving the nod to that rather bold idea of mixed bathing, as early as 1901. As a result – and despite the dire prophecies of the move's opponents – the fabric of society remained well this side of becoming irrevocably tattered.

Here — separated by nearly 50 years — are two views of one of the most timeless and best remembered of all seaside rituals: the donkey ride. Children down the years, though, have often been frustrated by the slow and sullen plod of these apparently very bored and put-upon creatures. This will have been particularly true of the boy at the centre of the Blackpool shot to the left. By the late 1950s, practically all of the most popular television programmes revolved around fast-moving horses: not just the imported American Westerns (*Wagon Train*, *Rawhide*, *The Lone Ranger*) but home-grown stuff such as *Robin Hood* too. His need to dig in spurs, kick up sand and leave his baby siblings standing is almost palpable; he would have loved it the way it was done at the beginning of the nineteenth century.

In those days, the donkeys in such terribly fashionable resorts as Brighton were mounted by elegant young ladies in Empire-line dresses. Both they and the servants chasing behind them used to whip up the animals into a frenzy, as well as frequently quite literally breakneck speed. To fall off — as was almost inevitable — was seen to be part of the fun, although broken ankles and arms were often the order of the day. Maybe the gentler pace we're all used to is preferable, on balance; parents, I'm sure, would agree.

Blackpool, incidentally, possibly more than all the other resorts, has always prided itself on not only preserving the best of the old traditions, such as donkey rides on the sands, but being first with all the new and ritzier trends. Not only was the jackpot struck with the famous tower and illuminations, but by the 1890s Blackpool was one of the very first places to market seaside rock in a big way. That vital and awful jawbreaking stuff in denture pink and disinfectant blue with the name of the resort written all the way through it, as if by magic. Blackpool rock was already a byword when, by the turn of the century, practically every other resort started selling its own.

These days, of course, in addition to the famous stripy columns, rock comes in the guise of just about everything from false teeth to babies' dummies, with an awful lot of unspeakable variety in between. There is no evidence that anyone actually eats it.

All sorts of disparate scenes from varying periods, but each serving to illustrate, in its own singular way, just how determined the British are to make the most of these rare and snatched sunlit hours.

The impromptu jazz band and tea dance (previous spread) is atypical, to say the least, but it looks great fun – even if the combo could maybe benefit from a string section, or possibly a trumpet to hit the high notes.

On these pages, and overleaf, we have depictions of a tradition far more usual: that of sitting on stones, and sucking in the ozone. The children in Littlehampton in the 1920s (left) seem quite literally beached; almost as if they have been recently shipwrecked, and are now awed and subdued by their long and perilous swim ashore. Far more likely, they are in between games, and maybe dreading the moment when once more they are to be divided into teams.

The impressive panorama below was photographed around the turn of the century at Whitby, North Yorkshire. The few intrepid youngsters who have ventured into the water are far outnumbered by the more cautious parents, nannies and aged relatives, who are standing idly by. The moated hillock of compacted sand in the foreground just hours earlier might have been a turreted fantasia to rival that at Lichtenstein, before the sea rushed up and over it, in its endless bid for reclamation. This is why each dawn the beach appears so utterly new again.

As for the stylish and bright young things over the page (class of 1930), despite the fact that they have plumped for the rockier end of Eastbourne, they really do seem to have the informal beach gathering off to a fine art. Not just the latest hairstyles and terribly *chic* and casually worn accessories – but even a portable gramophone. Maybe that's why they avoided sand. Heaven knows the recording would have been scratchy enough as it was.

If just one picture were needed to exemplify the truth that the seaside is good for you, this very well could be it.

Headgear. The seaside is very given to headgear, of one sort or another. The newspaper wimple (the examples above of 1950) used to be a common choice among those who lacked the sophistication to tie a knot in each of their commodious gent's hanky and slap that on their heads instead. People buy jokey hats with slogans at the seaside that elsewhere they would not be seen dead in. In the 1940s, paper sailor hats bearing the legend "Attaboy" were popular (and particularly *risqué* when worn by a girl). These gave way in the 1950s to fringed cowboy hats ("Kiss Me Quick" – the reverse reading "Squeeze Me Slow") and more latterly baseball caps and cricket hats emblazoned with any sort of rudeness under the sun.

All a far cry from the matrons to the right, of 1900. Not only do their amazing hats suggest winter in town, but they seem astonished too by the sight before their eyes: Eastbourne Pier, amid all that sea.

From Beach Huts
to Pavilions

Beach architecture – like the seaside itself – is all about having fun, but as usual the contrasts
are marked. Brightly painted stilted beach huts in the shadow of a grand uplit theatre, maybe just
round the corner from the sort of bandstand with pilasters and porticoes that will always recall
the glory days of panamas and parasols and thoroughly British music, leavened by the odd
Viennese waltz and possibly the hit of the moment. The whole point of these hugely disparate
structures, along with the mighty piers and promenades, was to provide diversion and
entertainment for all the family from dawn to dusk. And because this is the seaside we are talking
about, the architecture is of course rather quirky, and wholly peculiar to Britain's coastline.

This dawn shot of a beautifully maintained row of beach huts at Southwold, Suffolk (left) pretty well sums up the romance of the concept of owning one's very own private box in the greatest theatre of them all: the seaside, with its ever changing shifts in backdrop and lighting. Those below, at Wells-next-the-Sea, Norfolk, are built on stilts to cope with the vagaries of the tides, and very much recall the general design of nineteenth-century bathing machines – the forerunners of the beach hut. These were wheeled, and hauled into the sea either manually or by horses, the idea being that a lady could step into the water in her fantastically voluminous bathing dress, virtually unseen. This cumbersome machine was permanently "beached" as mixed bathing became the norm – obliging many men to don a costume for the first time, skinny-dipping having formerly been quite common.

Scarborough was Britain's very first seaside resort, this distinction by virtue of its having been the only one of the many fashionable mineral-spa towns of the early eighteenth century that happened to be built on the coast. This was at a time when it was popularly decreed that if you both drank the mineral water and bathed in the salty sea, your health would be boundless for just about ever.

On the left we can see a detail of the splendid ironwork and bandstand, and above, a more general view of their grand and rather wonderful setting. The 1880s were the heyday throughout Britain for the design and rapid proliferation of such glories as this, Scarborough being unique in having had no fewer than two of these very stylish rotunda, one at either end of the promenade. As you enjoyed your bracing constitutional along the front, the melody and cadence of one band would fade just as the ear took up the rousing chords of the next. Bracing, or what? Scarborough led the way too in the scale and quality of its other amenities, very much aiming for and achieving the carriage-trade sector of the market. By the end of the nineteenth century, it was popularly agreed that the theatre and musical entertainments to be had here were – along with those in Blackpool, Bournemouth and Eastbourne – the very best outside of London.

Municipal orchestras were founded, and drama and opera companies visited often and to great acclaim. Scarborough was also the site of one of the country's very first magnificent and grand hotels: The Grand, predictably enough, opened in 1867. On the previous page we have a packed-out and no-less-splendid promenade and bandstand at Eastbourne, c.1930 (*see also pages* 54–5).

The fine and dramatically uplit Art Deco theatre
at the end of the 700-foot-long Wellington Pier,
at Great Yarmouth, Norfolk. Originally built in 1853
as a tribute to the Iron Duke, it has certainly fared
better than Yarmouth's second pier, the Britannia.

This was opened just five years later, and within
months was cut in half by a sloop. In 1868, about
100 feet of it was accidentally towed out to sea
by a schooner – and during this century alone the
thing has burned down three times. But Yarmouth
loves both its piers, and these days each of them
is in very fine fettle indeed.

The town has long been a seaside favourite.
In Dickens' *David Copperfield*, young Peggotty
at one point passes the opinion that Yarmouth is
"upon the whole, the finest place in the Universe".
While this might be seen to be a little exaggerated,
the fans do seem to come back, year after year.

Here's a list of goodies available on the piers
in 1897: "Chocolate cream buns – two a penny;
apples – penny a bag; Yarmouth rock – penny
a box; lemonade – threepence a bottle; walnuts –
eight a penny; milk – penny a glass." Followed,
maybe, by a trip round the bay; or not.

The spectacular colours of the beach huts in Southwold, above, demonstrate how terribly well cared for these sought-after and increasingly expensive seaside havens always are. Southwold in Suffolk is one of the most traditional resorts, peace and tranquillity being the order of the day. Local estate agents report a constant demand for these huts, many of them maintaining a waiting list long enough to rival that of the most exclusive London club. "People see them as a retreat from the real world," says one. "You see the proud owners sitting in the porches in all weathers, just gazing out to sea and thinking their thoughts." And when they're not doing that, they are – in true British style – tending to their property.

Clearly, the alternation of bright primary colours is a result of serious consultation with the cooperative neighbours, roof felting being a common and shared preoccupation. It is not unusual for a hut on a prime promenade here to sell for up to £15,000, so there's also the investment factor to consider; although most are handed down from generation to generation. At Frinton, as may be seen from the picture on the right, the huts are a good deal less showy – and there you have Frinton in a nutshell. It is unique in being a "dry" resort: there are no pubs (although, at the time of writing, an application to open the very first is being hotly debated).

Visitors may only – modestly – partake of alcohol in hotels (if they are resident or dining) or the tennis club (unlikely, as one must be a member). Banned too are all the usual fun, frolics and indulgences that tend to be part and parcel of the seaside (including piers), much to the delight of the town's grandees, and the frustration of the resident youth. Very recently, the town's first fish and chip shop opened, its opponents having condemned it as the thin end of the wedge. But, with its gothic-lettered fascia proclaiming it to be "The Nice Fish and Chip Shop", it appears to be thriving.

Arguably one of the two most famous examples of seaside architecture: the Royal Pavilion. (For the other, see above: Blackpool Tower.) John Nash started work on his extravagant masterpiece in 1815, on the site of a far humbler residence acquired by George IV, then Prince Regent. As a result of the Regent's flamboyant hospitality, a humble coastal village was transformed into far and away the most fashionable resort in Britain, attracting scores of thousands of visitors annually, as it continues to do today.

The Regent's profligacy, however, many found breathtaking, including the wife of the then Russian Ambassador to England, who wrote in a letter: "How can one describe such a piece of architecture? The style is a mixture of Moorish, Tartar, Gothic and Chinese, and all in stone and iron. It is a whim which has already cost £700,000 and is still not fit to live in." This in 1820! Thirty years later, demolition was narrowly avoided by its purchase by the town commissioners for just £53,000, though its decline was steady and seemingly irreversible until 1945, when the newly formed Regency Society pledged its restoration.

There have been many setbacks over the decades: a fire in 1975; and the 1987 hurricane sent a minaret plunging through the dome and deep into the floor of the Music Room. But these days the splendid Brighton Pavilion is both magical and perfect.

The awesome journey up Blackpool Tower is not, as they say, for those of a nervous disposition – but this couple seems to be coping all right. Blackpool has always been bigger and brassier then anywhere else, and nothing exemplifies this so emphatically as the 500-foot-tall tower (*see also page* 87).

The Pleasure Beach – Britain's first permanent seaside amusement park – rose out of a tract of waste land on the South Shore – a rather dangerous place, by all accounts, frequented by gypsies. The tower was two years in the building and opened in 1884, by which time the piers and the glorious Golden Mile were already lit up by electricity.

This early commitment to the bright lights steadily grew until the 1920s, when the "Illuminations" proper came into being, and from then onwards, everyone has loved to come and be dazzled. In the 1920s too, Blackpool unveiled the largest swimming pool in the country, built at a cost of £100,000. Since that time, Blackpool has continued to vault from strength to strength, giving to the people (well – selling it to them, anyway) exactly what they want. Holiday makers who love Blackpool *really* love Blackpool – they simply cannot see the point of going anywhere else in the whole wide world.

This tight and sheltered cluster of buildings typifies Hastings, in Sussex (below and right). Seaside towns and villages began to be popular as holiday resorts only towards the end of the eighteenth century, when grand sea-facing terraces, crescents and keynote examples of coastal architecture began to be built. Before then, traditional ports and fishing villages such as Hastings had been constructed in a way that would now seem back to front. Houses were huddled in groups, facing away from the sea in an attempt at protection from the often ferocious storms in winter. In Hastings, the High Street ran inland, between the town's hallmark cliffs, and it was only later that cliff-top terraces came to be built in parallel to the coast, taking their lead from nearby Brighton.

Seen below are the tall net-drying huts, unique to Hastings. Although the town still has a fairly active fishing tradition, many of these huts are now converted into shops for the tourists. But Hastings has always been aware of this lucrative potential. As early as the 1880s, when fishing was the life-blood of the town, the gnarled and briny fishermen would rarely be too busy to find the time to spin out some fantastic seaman's yarn for the benefit of a credulous Londoner, all in exchange for a drink. This soon became a very profitable sideline, and many were the sou'westered old salts, overcharging wildly for fresh-caught fish or a trip in their boats, while their wives sold old nets and floats to prettify urban homes and gardens.

In the background below may be seen the vertiginous funicular railway – a combination of tram and cable-car – well known in other cliff-bound resorts, notably Bournemouth. These late nineteenth-century innovations were a sure-fire hit with the visitors – as was the proliferation of miniature railways – Hastings' version seen to the right.

All Work and No Play

Very very few resorts nowadays have anything in common with the modest fishing villages and
towns that spawned them (although a few places, such as Hastings retain some of the tradition).
But as the appeal of the seaside spread, so did all sorts of seasonal work arise: it takes a lot
of man hours to keep all those holiday-makers happy. Many of the jobs now are taken by students
on vacation, but it remains a mystery as to just what happened in the old days to all those
uniformed attendants, hawkers and open-air entertainers, once the season had ended.

Variations upon one of the most enduring British themes of all:
refreshments in general, and tea and ice-cream in particular. Overleaf
we have wholesale teas in the 1930s "at popular prices" on Brighton's
Palace Pier, while these holiday-makers above, in Ramsgate in 1945,
are more than happy to queue for their twopenny cup or, for the
serious tea drinker, one of the jugs on offer (see also page 107).

For sheer enterprise alone, though, this man on the right deserves
to make his fortune out of that box of Bailey's Ice-Cream. It is true
that the British in summer do not need much persuasion to buy
gallons, but to pull on waders and walk into the sea at Brighton
(where this picture was taken in 1939), and actually bring the luscious
stuff to the punters is truly inspired.

The two best-known northern resorts are represented here – Scarborough to the left and Blackpool (but of course) above. There are still many shoplets such as Mr Bradbury's establishment in virtually every major resort in Britain, and little will have changed since this picture of 1952. Save the prices: these days, you're just not going to get plaice and chips, tea, bread and butter for three shillings (15 pence). The ubiquitous burger, of course, is absent from the menu, and the bottles of pop are on shelves as opposed to in a fridge; though warm and flat drinks are a British tradition that many traders remain committed to, whether you like it or not.

The attractions at the Floral Hall look very enticing: not only the ventriloquist Peter Brough with that most famous dummy, Archie Andrews, but comedians too of the calibre of Ted Ray, Peter Sellers, Max Wall and Beryl Reid – to say nothing of the peerless tenor Josef Locke. Those were indeed the days, it very much would seem.

The rare view of South Beach, Blackpool, is quite misleading: were it not for the tower, one could well believe that here was just another ordinary and rather dull town, given over to fishing. Quite wrong: by the time this photograph was taken (c.1893) a ferris wheel to rival that on Coney Island was already in place; the highest-paid entertainers were packed out on both piers (Caruso earned £1,000 for just one concert at the Winter Gardens); and the better restaurants were serving 100 covers a night. Some of the earliest mechanical slot machines were crowded on the front (the explicit recreation of the Execution of Mary Queen of Scots a perennial and particular favourite).

But, cautions a town guide of the period: "Baths and pianos are the rule; good music and good singing are often indulged in, coarseness or vulgarity is strictly put down." These days, it's just maybe a little different.

Oh dear, oh dear, oh dear: while springtime 1947 in Brighton (above) sees the ritual and more-or-less constant refurbishment of the West Pier in readiness for the coming summer hoards, in Margate (left) later the same year, the season is already well and truly upon them – and it has turned out to be an unmitigated disaster: "wintry gales, biting cold and driving rain", to quote a report of the time.

But, look – we British didn't come through two World Wars (the most recent very fresh in the collective memory) solely in order to let a little thing like a wet July deter us from having a good time ... or so the unfortunate members of Arthur Illston's Margate Follies thought, anyway. The paying customers clearly decided otherwise. Three times a day the frolicsome octet had to face this howling void – but I bet each and every one was chipper to the end.

Beach entertainment such as this has long and noble tradition and (weather permitting) could usually be depended upon to draw an appreciative audience. While the very grandest resorts, such as Blackpool and Brighton, regularly hired the top entertainers of their day (opera singers and musicians at the turn of the century and beyond, pop stars and television comedians from the 1950s to date) and put at their disposal vast and palatial theatres, the humbler resorts made do with variations of the strolling player – the cacophony of conflicting barrel organs, it was generally agreed being far and away the most appalling.

Brass bands were popular, but before that came the ubiquitous "nigger minstrels" – blacked-up singers, banjo players and fiddlers, backed by concertinas and tambourines. All unthinkable now, of course, but in those days they were a vital and much-loved part of the scene.

It has to be faced that, in common with the world at large, some seaside jobs are inherently more glamorous than others. On the previous page, the young man at the centre is clearly enjoying being a fit and bronzed lifeguard in 1950 Newquay. He obviously has a pretty effective sideline going with the instruction of a bevy of local lovelies on the finer points of surfboarding. I think he would agree that as summer jobs go, this very much comes close to the head of the nice-work-if-you-can-get-it category.

Now glance if you will at our two uniformed officials, also of 1950, to the right and above. Both are working Brighton beach as well as the piers. But the fellow with his arms brimful of threepenny deckchair tickets, we may feel sure in assuming, very much appreciates his office,

as the gleaming cap badge and buttons amply make clear. He may not enjoy it to the extent of our lifeguard friend overleaf but nonetheless here is a man ready to do battle with the summer, come hell or high water. Woe betide any clever Dick, smart Alec or flash Harry seeking to save his threepenny bit for a surreptitious cornet and vacating the deckchair at the man's approach. He wasn't born yesterday: he's seen and heard it all, mate – so cough up, sonny, and look lively about it. The old chap above, though, is simply doing his job. "Don't blame me it's thruppence, love – blame the Corporation. I don't get the money: wish I did. Me? I'm just doing my job."

(In modern-day Brighton, overleaf, there seem to be fewer takers.)

KIPPERS
PAIRS
4'6

FROM
ROUGH

3/-
3/6
4/-
4/6

1/6
2/-
2/6

3/6

2/6
2/-

FRESH PRAWNS
1/-

FRESH
SHRIMPS
6
PER BAG

WINKLES
6 PER BAG

Mrs CO KES
FISH   ALER

And here we go again: another day, another scallop – with maybe a dozen or two winkles and a crab to take home to the wife ("as if you weren't crabby enough – joke! It's a joke: honestly, love, I'm only joking"). This particular stall, brimming with fresh-caught wonder, was captured at Scarborough in 1952 – and we really must pause a while to savour the effortless perfection of the shellfish-lover's attire. In the 1950s in Britain – for men, anyway – there was no such concept as leisure wear, or indeed summer wear: you simply put on a bit less (not much) of what you habitually wore, though maybe with a somewhat slacker commitment to coordination. Hence we have this delightful combination of a Prince of Wales jacket from one suit teamed with chalk-striped trousers from another, sufficiently rolled up to reveal that all-important touch of rakish nakedness – just enough to hint at abandon. Top this off with a houndstooth cap and

you were ready for anything. The paying customers above, by contrast, all seem to be decked out in their Sunday best, but then the acquisition of tea at any time – but most especially at the seaside – was always possessed of a quasi-religious undertone.

One can only wonder at people's reaction when first they set eyes on this fabulous mobile kiosk on Blackpool beach in the mid-1930s: could they have been out in the sun too long? Had their yearning for tea finally turned their minds so that they were seeing mirages? After a shock like that, the only solution is a bit of a sit down, and a nice cup of tea. The less publicised corollary to all this tea, and of course, is the need to rapidly locate the all-important public conveniences – with the ladies almost always generating yet another patient queue; but here was a useful time-filler until the time rolled round again for another lovely cup of tea.

All the Fun of the Fair

There are funfairs elsewhere, it is true, but nowhere but the seaside do you get the all-important salty tang in the air, the sudden gusts that always threaten to blow ladies' dresses right over their heads while they are suspended 30 feet in the air on some terrible contraption or other, both hands clutching tight the safety rail. And the dodgems – at every hairpin bend, you can thrill to the sensation of being about to shoot off the pier altogether and plummet into the sea. The British like a bit of fear, with their pleasure.

The woman above, in Southend in 1952, appears to be having a whale of a time – cheerfully passing over sixpence after sixpence in exchange for the sheer good fun of hurling wooden balls at coconuts, all of which have lodged snugly in their shies possibly for years. There is no record of anyone actually winning a coconut, but by the time you were about three shillings down, some sideshow operators would take

pity and dole out a goldfish in a plastic bag which – as simply anyone will tell you – just isn't the same thing at all. To the right, we have a wheel-load of more intrepid holiday-makers at Brighton in 1938, each of them having paid to be terrified in the age-old and traditional way. Blackpool was one of the very first resorts to put up a ferris wheel. Overleaf is the current quite awe-inspiring version, on Central Pier.

The rather smart twins to the left are in Blackpool in 1955. They must have just been to the fair (the chief source of all that roof insulation in Windolene pink they choose to call candy floss), and have maybe just bought tickets for the new hit comedy show "Love and Kisses". Spare a thought for the then hugely popular Arthur Askey, who had to perform the thing no less than twice nightly.

The attraction above must surely have seemed to be the acme of sophistication in 1954. Where else but Torquay ("The English Riviera") would one expect to find a glamorous re-enactment of the Monte Carlo Rally? It is a variation on the old "rolling a ball into a hole" game, everyone willing it to be a sure-fire winner so that they can bear home in triumph the glittering prizes.

And just look at what's on offer: a butter dish, a teapot, a box of spoons! It fair makes you dizzy. Another variation of this was based around a perpetually grinning clown: you had to propel a ball into his mouth and down his throat, whereupon it would emerge somewhat disconcertingly from his stomach and idly roll into the wrong hole altogether. After half-a-crown's worth of this lark, you yearned to knock that stupid grin off his face, but all you actually did was slope off and lose some more money on yet another variation of the same old thing. The Monte Carlo Rally people were taking no chances. It says on the notice: "Any player winning twice in succession on the same table will please change tables. Thank you." What a nerve; never get that box of spoons, now.

Pictured here and overleaf are three entertainments guaranteed
to make you heartily regret having had a last toffee apple on top
of the cornet, peppermint rock and all that candy floss.

The helter-skelter at Hunstanton in Norfolk, overleaf, is maybe not
quite so heave-inducing, given that one's heart-stopping gyratory
descent is, at least, quite mercifully brief. But the forms of torture on
these pages always seemed to last for ever. No doubt the sailors
above, in Southend in 1945, are enjoying demonstrating to the popsies
not just their sea legs, but also the enviable ability to subdue their
rebellious stomachs while in the throes of the severest pitching and
tossing. But the girls too, to be fair, are putting a jolly brave face on it.
It is likely that these two couples will already have done the helter-

skelter and the ghost train (hugging in the dark as skeletons rattled
their bones – the lads just loving it when the girls started screaming).

Eventually, the ultimate will just have to be conquered: the big
dipper, such as this terror-making example to the right in 1950
Blackpool. This particular section is named after a jump at Aintree
racecourse, but you would almost prefer to be on a horse in the
Grand National than this awful thing. Some big dippers were called
water chutes – the final plummet culminating in a shallow reservoir,
this allowing you totter away afterwards not just with your insides
turned to jelly, but with the added bonus of being soaked to the skin.
All the fun of the fair! (One does hope that this dipper is closed:
otherwise those maintenance men are in for a big surprise.)

This sort of macho-machine – to the left on Brighton Pier in 1950 – has all but vanished, these days. There were "Test Your Strength" machines too: all to do with squeezing handles as hard as you could. (Many were the strained expressions and bursting blood vessels as he-men strove to outdo each other and impress to bits the young son – or, of course, the girl.) Grown men of a much earlier era would would derive similar kicks from bashing a huge button with a vast wooden mallet, the idea being to propel some sort of gizmo up the full height of a vertical shaft in order to ring the bell at the top. ("Give the man a cigar!")

Nowadays, this lust for power is largely catered to by virtual-reality machines, which enable the would-be Grand Prix champion to race his Porsche down an increasingly serpentine highway, and try not to flatten too many innocent pedestrians. Shooting down war-planes is also regarded fondly, as is the sinking of battleships. Well, boys will be boys, you know, and judging from the picture to the left, you're never too young to take those early first steps down the road to pugilism. Probably the lad would have infinitely preferred to go on the blissfully gentle roundabout above. The little fellow in the foreground is clearly and justly proud of having been first to bag the tank. (No one ever wanted to be on the top deck of the buses, obviously – up there you couldn't *drive* the thing.)

Overleaf is a knot of somewhat older children – genuine teddy boys of the 1956 variety, working the slots on Canvey Island. Two things leap to the eye, here: the cool and elongated cut of the boy's Edwardian drape jacket, and the entirely unconnected fact that the gaming machines back then resembled nothing so much as similarly Edwardian bedroom furniture.

It's those girls again! On page 102, the blonde on the left of the picture above is delving into her handbag for the threepenny hire of a deckchair. Here – further along Brighton Pier that summer of 1950 – she is investing in something a good deal more fun. The fact that she appears to be receiving a prize before actually chucking her dart appears a bit fishy, though. There are few known precedents of anyone winning anything even *afterwards*: for the simple reason that not only were dart points at the funfair both blunt and delicately curved (their ravaged flights of no use whatsoever). But the dartboards themselves had the air of being fashioned from highly resilient India rubber, in order to guarantee maximum bounce. Sometimes one was asked to throw the darts at pegged-out playing cards. The tally one was supposed to achieve always appeared to be laughably easy, but there was always some fantastically arcane small print that made sure that his was never the case. The odd thing was that although winning just anything at all was the biggest kick of all, coming nowhere close seemed pretty good fun as well (or so one had to keep telling oneself).

The enterprising milliner to the right (same pier, same year) is not herself tempted to emulate a policeman or a cowboy, sticking in time-honoured tradition to what seems to be a tea towel. All those hats will blow off anyway, when the boys climb aboard the huge and gorgeous Brighton carousel – seen overleaf, spinning thrillingly.

Index

AUTHOR ACKNOWLEDGEMENTS
The author would like to thank the following for their contributions in various capacities to the completion of this book: Clare Gouldstone, Hilary Lumsden, Susie Brumfitt, Tony Lynn, Gaye Allen, Martin Lovelock and Joe Cornish, for his wonderful colour pictures. Finally, my agent Giles Gordon and commissioning editor at Mitchell Beazley, Margaret Little: thanks for making the connection.
With thanks to John Murray (Publishers) Ltd for excerpts used from John Betjeman's *Beside the Seaside*.

PICTURE CREDITS
Jason Bell back flap, top.
Bridgeman Art Library/Donald McGill 7.
Joe Cornish back flap, bottom, endpapers, 2-3, 6, 10, 11, 14-15, 18-19 bottom, 19 top, 22-23, 26, 27, 30-31, 31 right, 34-35, 54 left, 54-55 right, 64-65, 76-77 bottom, 77 top, 80, 81, 82-83, 84 top, 85 bottom, 86 left, 87 right, 90-91 bottom, 91 top, 104-105, 110-111, 116-117, 124.
Hulton Getty Picture Collection front cover bottom, back cover, bottom, 4-5, 8, 9, 12, 13, 16-17, 17 right, 20-21, 24, 25, 28, 29, 32, 33, 36, 37, 38 left, 38-39, 40-41 left, 41-42 right, 42-43, 44-45, 46, 47, 48 left, 48-49 right, 50-51, 52, 53, 56-57, 58 left, 58-59 right, 60, 61, 62-63, 63 right, 66 top, 66-67 bottom, 68-69, 70 top, 70-71 bottom, 72-73, 74 top, 74-75 bottom, 78-79, 88-89, 92, 93, 94-95, 96, 97, 98, 99, 100-101, 102, 103, 106, 107, 108, 109, 112, 113, 114, 115, 118, 119, 120-121, 122, 122-123, 128.
Graeme Peacock front cover top, back cover, top.

And so … the last evening of the holiday has finally come. It was a long, sunny day on the pier. You bought lots of sticks of rock to bring back home, your photograph was taken while your head poked through a hole in a brightly-coloured and very tubby torso straining from within a one-piece striped costume. You looked into distorting mirrors and became a dwarf and a beanpole with a foot-wide mouth. You very nearly won a cuddly toy on the mechanical crane – it just slipped off at the very last moment. A palm reader told you you would have a long and happy life, be rich, have many children … but they're closing the pier, now – and it's just turned a little bit chilly. Must get away before the last of the lights winks out. You'll be back next year … but until then, goodnight.